The Thatcher Papers

an exposé of the secret face of the Conservative
government, based on information received by

Alistair Beaton & Andy Hamilton

NEW ENGLISH LIBRARY
TIMES MIRROR

A New English Library Original Publication,
1980

First NEL Paperback Edition, October 1980

NEL Books are published by
New English Library Limited,
Barnard's Inn, Holborn,
London EC1N 2JR.

Made and printed in Great Britain by
Hunt Barnard Web Offset, Aylesbury

0 450 05129 3

On a damp, drizzly evening in September 1979, while waiting for the 7.42 train from Victoria to Herne Hill, we were approached by a gaunt, stooped figure, his coat collar turned up against the chill of the early autumn. Before either of us had time to react, he had thrust a large buff envelope at us. He whispered hurriedly "Here, take this. It's up to you now", then melted away into the greyness of Victoria Station. At first we dismissed this man as a harmless eccentric, or perhaps a practical joker. Even after reading the contents of the envelope we remained somewhat sceptical.

However, subsequent contacts with this mysterious individual, who only ever referred to himself as 'Hermes', convinced us that we were being entrusted with a collection of secret and highly sensitive official documents which, taken together, added up to probably the most sensational and damning leak in the history of any British government. We have called them 'The Thatcher Papers'. In the pages that follow, they are laid out in the order that we received them from 'Hermes'. They begin with the contents of that first innocuous-looking buff envelope – a document that gives a remarkable insight into Mrs Thatcher's ability to ensure the total loyalty of her Cabinet colleagues.

Andy Hamilton & Alistair Beaton

INSTRUCTIONS
TO CABINET MINISTERS

These instructions to be carried
out *to the letter* at all times.

General

You are privileged to have been granted a position of responsibility in the most forward-looking government since 1506. Such privilege carries certain obligations towards your leader: principally proper conduct, blind obedience, and fear.

Dress

Uniform will be worn at all times. Uniform consists of a grey suit (preferably a sober stripe), patent shoes, trousers with knee-pads for consultations with P.M. For Cabinet meetings *identity tags must be worn* for reasons of security and to inform the P.M. to whom she is talking. In the event of a woman Minister being appointed to the Cabinet she will attire herself with suitable restraint. Ministers for Consumer Affairs should not wear tons of garish costume jewellery nor generally resemble an adventure playground.

Speech

Ministers' speeches should be as vague and as uninteresting as possible. This is to encourage public indifference and apathy. Interesting words may only be used when they are adjectival and relate to Trade Unions. Sentences should be left unfinished. The use of certain words is forbidden (see Glossary). All speeches to be given in public must be approved by the P.M. Ministers unclear as to exactly what it is they are trying to say should affect a speech defect. (Seek advice from Norman St. John Stevas, Tel: 01-881-1342 and ask for Bunny.)

Conduct

The entire Cabinet must at all times abide by the rule of 'collective responsibility': a democratic system whereby the P.M. takes a decision and you all agree with it. The P.M.'s decision is final. Ministers caught whining in private will be thrashed. There will be no resignations, unless requested by the P.M. Those attempting to leave the organisation without consent will receive two warnings, the first in the form of a written censure, the second in the form of a horse's head in their bed. Sacked Ministers will not bellyache to the Press (such action will count against your peerage rating).

Personal Life

To avoid scandal, Ministers will be driven to and from their work in closed vans. The P.M. will take a very dim view of any Ministers caught cruising on Hampstead Heath.

Do's and Don'ts

Do
– take every opportunity to praise the courage of your Leader.
– take every opportunity to insult the French.
– try to remember the name of your constituency.
– try to be photographed climbing into helicopters.
(Note: Ministers for Health should always say nice things about nurses.)

Do Not
– blush if caught lying.
– sleep with Polish actresses who know Nigel Dempster.
– sleep with Nigel Dempster.
– tell the Blair Peach joke in public.

Non – Intervention
The most important part of any
Minister's job is non-intervention.
The art of non-intervention is a
difficult one and should be
practised as often as possible, using
the following non-intervention
drill.

Non-intervention drill
In the event of an emergency such
as a national strike in a vital
service, or the collapse of an entire
industry, this is what to do.

　　1. Sit still and do nothing.

2. Sit still and do nothing.

3. Express concern.

OH
DEAR

4. Sit still and do nothing a bit more.

5. Arrange to see leaders of all parties concerned.

6. Then sit still
   and do nothing.

7. Make a cup of tea.

8. Sit still and do nothing (until
   market forces find their natural
   level).

REMEMBER
if all else fails, *sit still and do
nothing*.

IMPORTANT:
It is worth remembering how to sit
still and do nothing in the dark in
case of a national power strike.

How To Snub Ted Heath

1. If approached by Ted Heath, remain calm.

2. When hand-shake seems imminent, turn away.

3. If he persists in trying to make conversation, make your position clear.

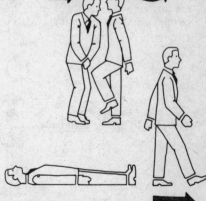

4. Leave

How to Annoy a Trade Union Leader

1. Arrange a meeting with him.

2. Don't turn up.

3. Arrange another meeting.

4. When he arrives, make sure you are surrounded by crates of champagne. Don't offer him any.

5. Talk about the need for everyone to tighten their belts.

6. Lecture him on the causes of inflation.

7. Tell him his men are overpaid as it is.

8. Stress how everyone has to make sacrifices.

9. Tell him to go away.

GLOSSARY

Do *NOT* Use:	Use *INSTEAD:*
Employment............................	Temporary non-redundancy.
Foreign policy	Rolling back the Soviet threat.
The National Health Service	The crumbling monolith of state medicine.
Widespread factory closures	Squeezing inflation out of the system.
Reintroduction of the death penalty.....................................	Responding to the groundswell of deep-rooted public opinion.
Remaining in the EEC	Refusing to be stampeded by the transient drift of public opinion.
A 5% wage increase...................	Holding the country to ransom.
Getting the sack........................	Self-inflicted unemployment
Going without food	Living within your means.
A strike	A lemming-like urge for self-destruction.
Ignoring women's rights..............	Learning to walk before you can run.
Withholding payments from the EEC	Shouldering the burden equally.
Demanding a ten-billion pound refund from the EEC	Shouldering the burden equally.
Sending strikers to Botany Bay.....	Mobility of labour
Secondary picketing...................	The end of civilisation as we know it.

24th October 1979

At this stage a number of vital questions about our informant remained unanswered. Was he a reliable source? And if so, would he make contact again? Another buff envelope, this time sent through the post, dispelled our doubts. It contained four documents and a note saying

"Witness the shape of things to come
–Hermes."

The documents present an alarming picture of the government's intentions in the fields of energy, education, and devolution, as well as containing a list of proposed legislation which goes far beyond anything yet revealed to the British public.

Civil Service Department
Whitehall London SW1A 2AZ

The Prime Minister
10 Downing Street
London SW 1

Your reference
AOS/DFM
Our reference
SG/28/LM/08
Date: 8th October 1979

Dear Prime Minister,

Attached are the think-tank's ideas on
devolutionary possibilities. The think-
tank feels they are eminently feasible
in the present social context. Each
option is detailed individually and we
feel they present viable alternatives to
the original plan to use Northern Ireland,
Scotland and Wales as nuclear dustbins.

Thorneycroft

P.S. Hope Denis' trouble is better.

ENCS

THE ADVISORY COMMITTEE

Report (Confidential) on:

DEVOLUTION

Members of the Advisory Committee

Chairman: Lord Thorneycroft

Lord Hailsham
Lord Home
Angus Maude, M.P.
Sir Douglas Bader
Mark Thatcher
Sir Harold Wilson
'Spats' Lorenzetti
Hughie Greene
Billy Smart
Buster Mottram
Tommy Docherty

PROPOSAL 'A'

WALES

The utilisation of Wales as a Museum of Industrial Archaeology.

Advantages:

1: It would take very little to convert Wales into a Museum of Industrial Archaeology. All we need do is allow the present trend to continue for about another three weeks.

2: If the entrance fee for the Museum were £68 per head then Wales could be rendered economically viable, thereby ceasing to be a burden on Britain.

3: Jobs could be created for the indigenous population, serving teas and selling hot-dogs, T-shirts and 'I have seen the furnaces of Port Talbot' car-stickers.

4: As a novelty attraction, one of the steelworks could be kept in working order. (Needless to say this would be purely for purposes of historical interest, no steel would actually be produced.)

5: Swansea could be used as a foyer.

6: There could be special exhibitions of particular aspects of Welsh Industrial History, e.g. at noon every day visitors could witness a lock-out at a foundry, at 3 p.m., a re-enactment of the Tonypandy massacre, at 5.30 a two-hour concert of rousing Welsh music from the Massed Bands of the Unemployed. Plus, of course, singing. (Although widescale redundancies have affected the quality of Welsh singing, so it might be necessary to use tapes.) Evening attractions could include a 'son-et-lumière' pit disaster.

Disadvantages

(handwritten, top right) Not relevant M.T. ←

1: The Welsh might object.

2: Cardiff is not yet sufficiently dilapidated. Some demolition would have to be carried out. (Perhaps Welsh terrorists could be conned into burning bits down for us.)

Conclusion

On balance we feel that this scheme presents an acceptable solution to the Welsh problem. Other suggestions were considered, such as turning Wales into a car park, using it for germ research or simply fencing it off and ignoring it. These, however, were dismissed as being on the negative side.

(handwritten) Yes to all this. Suggest start printing brochures now. M.T.

PROPOSAL 'B'

SCOTLAND

The conversion of Scotland into 'Jockoland' –
an exciting new Safari Park:

Advantages

1: The Scots, roaming free in their natural habitat, are colourful, volatile creatures and would, we feel sure, attract many foreign visitors.

2: The cost of keeping the Scots would be very low as the tourists would throw them peanuts.

3: A scheme like this would help save the Scot from extinction.

4: A high, electrified fence, running the length of Hadrian's Wall, would give the Scots a long-sought-after feeling of independence.

Disadvantages

1: Obviously the big problem with 'Jockoland' would be *the safety of the tourists*. Signs would have to be displayed urging visitors to stay in their vehicles at all times and to keep their car windows firmly closed. Visitors who got into trouble would sound their horns till wardens (all with at least 3 years experience in Glasgow) came to their aid. All these precautions (plus the aforementioned electric fence) would increase the cost of the project.

2: Money would have to be spent on improving Scottish roads so that they could bear traffic.

3: Sir Alec Douglas-Home would be unable to travel south.

Conclusion

↖ Enter this under 'Advantages'
M.T

Again, we see this as the most sensible way of putting Scotland to use. Other schemes considered included creating the world's first 968-hole golf-course, storing Cruise missiles in it and just concreting over the lot. The great commercial possibilities of 'Jockoland', however, seem too good to miss.

Yes, in principle.
Not keen on the Scots getting free peanuts
M.T.

PROPOSAL 'C'

NORTHERN IRELAND

Putting Northern Ireland up for auction.

Advantages

1: The tragedy of Northern Ireland has haunted British Home Policy since 900 A.D. An insuperable enigma, the Irish problem has cost thousands of innocent lives throughout the blood-stained span of the ages. In brief, it's time we got shot of it.

2: The money we get from auctioning off Northern Ireland could be ploughed into setting up 'Jockoland'.

3: Such a scheme would set a useful precedent. (i.e. Humberside)

4: Ian Paisley would lose his seat in the House.

5: We could encourage bidders to take some of the more 'volatile' border counties off our hands by offering favourable discounts and 'special offers', e.g. a free set of tumblers with County Armagh.

Disadvantages

1: Some bits of Northern Ireland would not fetch very much as there's very little of them left.

2: Without Northern Ireland, where would we get our cheap labour from?

3: Who would we laugh at?

Conclusion

The pros and cons of this scheme are, it is true, much more evenly balanced. We feel, however, that 'Advantage (1)' far outweighs all other considerations. We urge this scheme to be adopted.

No !!
Ireland to go on being used as
Army Counter-Terrorist Training Ground

M.T.

CONSERVATIVE BOARD OF EXAMINERS

SUBJECT: Essential Basics.

Level: Ordinary

The candidate has **five minutes** *to finish this paper and then go out in the big wide world. Candidates who do not pass will be sent to Borstal.*
All *sections to be attempted.*
Each candidate will take it in turns to use the school pencil.

QUESTIONS

Section A: 'Rithmetic

1) If it takes 1 Minister four days to close 2 hospitals, how long would it take 3 Ministers to close 16?

2) Express the total of Britain's population as a percentage of its unemployed.

3) Using the 'Howe method' of new maths, show how $2+2=5.164$

Section B: 'Riting

4) Using not more than eight words, write an imaginative sentence on one of the following topics:

   a) Describe what you would have done in your summer holiday if you'd been able to afford one.

   b) Write an imaginary letter to your local DHSS office, informing them that your father is a Social Security scrounger.

   c) A day in the life of a tax exile.

Section C: Reading

5) Name a book (a comic will do).

Section D: History

6) "Margaret Thatcher – genius or deity?" Discuss.

7) "The finest woman P.M. since Neville Chamberlain." Is this a fair assessment of Margaret Thatcher?

8) Compare, with examples, the growth of trade unionism with the spread of the bubonic plague.

Section E: Geography

9) Draw a map of Russia, showing all the towns big enough to be worth eliminating.

Section F: French

10) Write, in French, a short composition telling Giscard d'Estaing exactly where he can stick his butter mountain. (Extra marks will be awarded for originality.)

Section G: Multiple Choice

11) When you have finished this exam, do you have any hope of getting a job? (Tick appropriate box).

☐ No.
☐ No.
☐ Not an earthly.
☐ Possibly. My father is a Mason.

Official report

ENERGY

The Future of North Sea Oil

Our enquiry into the future of North Sea Oil revealed three disturbing trends:

1. North Sea Oil ran out two years ago.
(Labour kept it a secret in case it cost them the election.)

2. The current supply of North Sea Oil is, in fact, shipped from Saudi Arabia in barrels marked 'North Sea Oil'.

3. The Saudis think this is very funny and keep mentioning it to other Arabs at parties.

Our enquiry therefore looked into possible alternative methods of energy creation and arrived at the following proposals:

1. Treadmill Power

This could harness the unemployed as a source of endless energy. Calculating at 16 persons per treadmill, Britain could soon have 125,000 units in operation. These would generate enough power to light a town of the size that, say, Corby used to be.

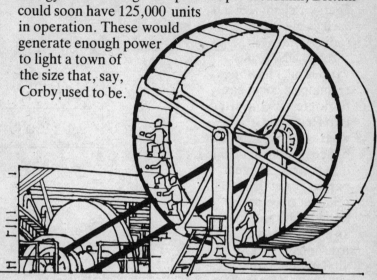

2. Recyclables

Already many materials are being recycled and converted into energy.

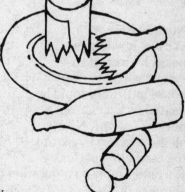

One valuable source of recyclable energy, however, is being largely neglected....

3. The Human Body

The human body contains a variety of energy-rich ingredients, such as phosphorus, sodium, nitrogen, carbon, DNA, and various oils. Existing crematoria could easily be discreetly converted into Recycling Centres where cadavers could be boiled down and distilled into their constituent parts. (Note: the relatives need never know.) This would put an end to an irresponsible waste of vital national resources. Similarly, deceased 'at rest' in cemeteries could be reclaimed and then processed.

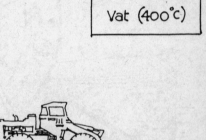

Vat (400°c)

4. Nuclear Energy

We feel it would be possible to create a system whereby every house in Britain could be heated by a leak from a nuclear reactor. Nearly all the reactors in use at the moment have leaks. It would simply be a question of moving all the houses closer to the reactors. (Which would be a lot cheaper than repairing the leaks.)

To all Ministers

Enclosed legislation to be passed at the earliest possible opportunity.

No arguments please

M.T.

IMPENDING LEGISLATION

DEFENCE

The Voluntary Conscription Act
All able-bodied adults between the ages of 12 and 78 to be offered the opportunity of enlisting in Her Majesty's forces. Those who decline will suffer no consequences, other than being put to work in munitions factories. A special government recruiting drive will be mounted to attract young men into the forces. (see 'Press Gang Act')

Nuclear Equalisation Act
This will empower the government to retaliate immediately against any act of nuclear hostility. Under this measure, the government will enjoy discretionary powers whereby it can retaliate first.

The Press Gang Act
(see Voluntary Conscription Act)

HOME AFFAIRS

Information Act
All mention in the media of the colony previously known as Northern Ireland to cease and the aforementioned province to be henceforth referred to as Nicaragua.

CIVIL RIGHTS

The Revised Sex Discrimination Act
Action on equal pay: If, when doing jobs of an equivalent nature, men should be found to be receiving a higher wage than women, then the men's wages will be lowered accordingly until parity is achieved.

Basic Rights Act
This Act will once and for all safeguard, under law, a citizen's inviolable right to keep a goldfish.

Social Security Investigators Control Act
This will restrict the activities of Social Security officials investigating cases of co-habitation by female claimants. Investigators' powers will be limited to entering premises without permission, confiscating personal documents, examining stains in laundry, and taking vaginal smears.

THE CONSTITUTION

The Mandatory Referendum Act
Referenda to be mandatory on issues where the country agrees with the Prime Minister but Parliament does not. e.g.: ejecting the French from the EEC, castrating football hooligans, hanging most people, etc.

LAW AND ORDER

Suspected Persons Act
An attempt to clear up the unfortunate ambiguities surrounding the so-called 'SUS' laws. Under this revision, police will be entitled to arrest anyone suspected of being about to be arrested.

Demonstrator Safety Act
People with thin skulls will be barred from attending demonstrations.

THE ECONOMY

Work Incentives Act
This will introduce widespread incentives to work, such as means tests, workhouses, confiscation of offspring, and bamboo under the fingernails.

Pensioners Relief Act
Designed to ensure that *the old must not suffer.* The aged will receive favourable discounts on essential goods, such as venison, contraceptives, iguanas, myrrh, Harrier Jump Jets, and chandeliers.

Relief Payments Act
This will empower the government to suspend all Social Security payments when it is necessary to the national economy, or when the month has an 'R' in it.

National Lottery Act
The introduction of an annual National Lottery, with tickets selling at £3. The winner will receive the only council house built that year.

Voluntary Pay Restraint Act
Whilst not instituting a formal policy of pay restraint, (which would be interventionist) employers will be given various suggestions for imposing voluntary restraint on wages, such as asking workers if they'd mind forgoing their wages this week, 'accidentally' forgetting to sign pay-cheques or arranging for employees to be relieved of their wage-packets by company pickpockets. Those firms failing to implement the measures to be blacklisted.

EDUCATION

Viable Schooling Act
Introduction of 'Pay As You Learn' scheme, whereby all teachers are fitted with meters and children pay by the hour. No lessons will be permitted on a credit basis. Children falling behind with payments to be jeered at during assembly.

INDUSTRIAL RELATIONS

Picketing Control Act
All pickets to be required to possess a 'Picketing Licence', obtainable from the 'Picket Licensing Centre, Swansea'. All those applying will simply have to present a personal photograph signed by a person of standing, thirteen references, an insurance certificate covering the picket for 'Third Party, Fire and Lorry Wheels', a blood sample (2 gallons), a typed thesis on 'Recurrent Imagery in Omar Khayyam', and the forelock of a unicorn.

GENERAL

The Anti-Frivolity Act
To create the right atmosphere of social responsibility, this Act will introduce a new range of offences, including 'Frivolous Behaviour', 'Trivial Bodily Harm', 'Drunk in charge of a silly giggle', 'Possession of a Dangerous Joke' and 'Breach of the Seriousness'.

Having heard nothing from 'Hermes' for almost eight weeks, we received an unexpected Christmas present: a gift-wrapped package containing another buff envelope, this time marked "Happy Christmas—Hermes". The sheer diversity of the data presented to us indicated beyond any doubt that we were dealing with a source so well placed that he could gain access to information ranging from a departmental circular to the personal correspondence of the Prime Minister.

This batch of documents reveals Saatchi & Saatchi's central role in the presentation of Conservative policies, and also includes one document which frankly remains a mystery to us. We can only assume it to be the result of a pre-election screening of Mrs Thatcher by influential elements within the Intelligence Services.

3rd November 1979

Dear PM,

Here's a draft of the poem
you commissioned to mark the
anniversary of your coming
to power.

If it doesn't seem immodest,
I do think the poem is quite
a jolly little number,
combining a certain respect
with an irrepressible 'joie
de vivre'.

I do hope you like it.

Yours sincerely,

Betgers

Sir John Betjeman

P.S. How many more bloody
     poems do I have to write
     before my peerage comes
     through?

THE VISION OF NO. 10

by Sir John Betjeman

Through the streets of London crawling,
Comes a number twenty-four,
Past the slums so quaintly sprawling,
All the way to Maggie's door.

Past the people buying and selling
Goes the dear old twenty-four,
Past the dole queues gently swelling,
All the way to Maggie's door.

Maggie T, Oh Maggie T,
Is it, could it,
Can it be?
Break my heart
But let me see
A glimpse, one glimpse of Maggie T.

From the bus I praise the people,
Enterprise has set them free.
I spot the soaring Gothic steeple
- That didn't need the NEB.

Through the Circus, past the Dilly,
(See the prostitutes get fined),
But I have got - it may sound silly -
A different lady on my mind.

Maggie T, Oh Maggie T,
Can I hope that
You'll love me?
Oh long indeed
Eternit-ee
Without the touch of Maggie T.

Past the Minis, past the Rolls,
Down through old Trafalgar Square.
Past the SPG patrols
And the Drug Squad, everywhere.

Then a sense of glory caught me,
Downing Street came into sight.
There lives Maggie, she who taught me
Left is wrong and Right is Right.

Maggie T, Oh Maggie T,
Were you made
For men to see?
Will you spare
One kiss for me?
A kiss, one kiss, dear Maggie T?

Past the Cenotaph inviting,
Past the bobby at the door,
Oh gosh...
This poem's so exciting
I really can't write any more.

&Saatchi Saatchi

Advertising
Consultants

by appointment to the
Prime Minister

14th November 1979

Dear Prime Minister,

As requested, we enclose an outline of our research
and proposals on the promotion of the Nuclear
Conflict Enhancement Campaign.

As you will see, our proposals are still at an early
stage and will require further discussion and refine-
ment before detailed campaign planning can be com-
menced.

We enclose our bill for £493,745 (including VAT).
We respectfully request that this be paid in full
prior to any outbreak of World War III.

Yours faithfully,

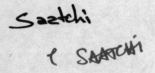

Campaign Proposals

Subject: Nuclear War

A. Public Attitudes

A survey of public attitudes has revealed that many people adopt a negative posture over the prospect of nuclear war. Typical phrases used by those interviewed were:
"I don't want to die."
"Nobody would win the next war."
"Better red than dead"
and
"Why the hell should I fry for that bitch?"

This sort of narrow response is deeply rooted in the British public mind. However, in the United States, our New York branch's slogan 'Let's nuke the Ayatollah now' has met with great success, and there is essentially no reason why a concerted campaign in Britain should not generate the same kind of encouraging response.

B. Campaign Management

Initial analysis suggests that a triple-stranded initiative is likely to prove most effective:

Strand One: Horror Minimalisation

The main aim of this initiative would be to induce in the public mind the feeling that thermo-nuclear conflict would be *just another war*.

An ongoing survival credibility campaign would generate the feeling that while a number of people might die, there would also be a *large number of survivors*. To heighten public receptivity to this promotion, government Ministers must adopt a new terminological posture when addressing the problem. Thus, for example:

a) The term 'Megadeath' should be dropped and replaced by 'megalife', as in: "There would be a high megalife count".
b) The term 'nuclear war' should be replaced by the term 'serious conflict', as in: "We may be forced to declare serious conflict on the Soviet Union".
c) The term 'pre-emptive strike' should be dropped and replaced by the term 'alert posture', as in: "Let's sneak in an alert posture when the Russians aren't looking".

Strand Two: Tension Marketing

The generation of an ongoing tension scenario is an essential component of the overall campaign.

Various factors already present in the existing marketing arena lend themselves to a successful campaign which has every chance of penetrating all socio-economic classes.

Factors to be exploited include:

a) The Soviet threat. This can be built up using both traditional methods, such as easily-written articles by George Feifer in the *Sunday Times,* and more commercially upfront tactics, such as a series of very fat Russian women on page three of the *Sun.*

b) Rejection of peace proposals by foreign powers. Ministers should offer arms limitations talks linked to a set of apparently simple pre-conditions: e.g.: The Soviet Union must first demonstrate its sincerity by either

  (i) dismantling its health service
   or
  (ii) withdrawing all Soviet troops from Afghanistan, Angola, and Russia.

Strand Three: Civil Defence Enhancement Scenario

The generation of a viable civil defence consciousness in the public mind would serve as a useful and easily-managed adjunct to Horror Minimalisation and Tension Marketing.

A viable civil defence scenario need not actually involve the provision of nuclear shelters for the general populace, as this would prove prohibitively expensive. However, research reveals a widespread public resistance to the ideal of dying for one's country when it is known that nuclear shelters are available for the government and leading public figures. To overcome this passive market resistance, the following techniques might be adopted:

a) The harnessing of unemployed school-leavers in Youth Employment Schemes, using them to build Community Shelters out of old table-tops, used bandages and so on. These would of course be totally useless in the event of a nuclear war, but they would provide a focal point for public participation in the coming conflict. Further thought might be given to the idea of linking the payment of unemployment benefit to compulsory participation in this kind of voluntary work.

b) The distribution of approximately ten million black and yellow signs saying 'There is a public fallout shelter underneath this building'. Research indicates that people will believe this.

Note:
It is vital that there is no public discussion of the shelter arrangements for the Royal Family. In particular, it could prove a negative campaign input to reveal the existence of twenty years supply of Chateau Lafitte in the shelters under Buckingham Palace.

Saatchi & Saatchi
October 1979

DHSS CIRCULAR No. 18492/B31/H563c.
'Responsibility & Health'.

Department of Health & Social Security

From: Dr Gerard Vaughan.
To: Doctors, Consultants, Surgeons.

It has come to the Department's attention
that NHS patients are being misled about
their rights. This is good as far as it
goes, but further efforts <u>must</u> be made to
present the private option in a favourable light. A large number of patients
are still being given free treatment and
are making use of NHS prescriptions (due
to go up to £4.75 next October, but still
absurdly cheap).

It is your professional duty to ensure
the most effective use of limited resources. All staff are urged to read
carefully the documents enclosed with
this circular, viz:
  a) A diagrammatic guide to consult-
     ation procedures.
  b) A transcript of a model consult-
     ation which falls fully within
     the Department's guidelines
     'Responsibility & Health'.

Dr Gerard Vaughan

Consultations: A DHSS Guide for Doctors

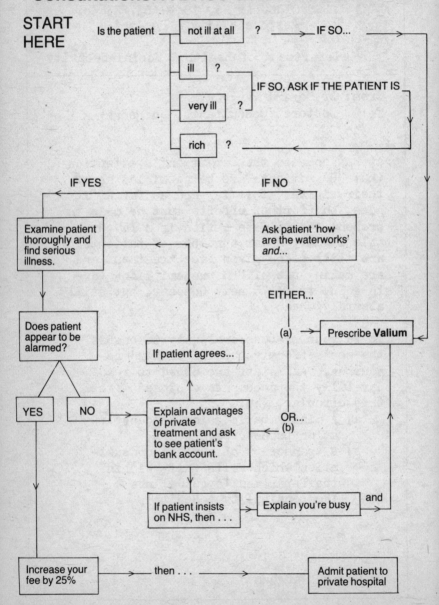

DHSS 'RESPONSIBILITY & HEALTH'

Model consultation. **Note and copy.**

Doctor: Ah, good morning, Mrs Smith.

Patient: Good morning, Doctor.

Doctor: And what seems to be the trouble?

Patient: Well, Doctor, I've got this terrible pain in . . .

Doctor: In BUPA?

Patient: No, in the chest, just here.

Doctor: But you want to go private?

Patient: Well, actually, I was hoping. . .

Doctor: Hoping to live? Well that means going private, you know. (DOCTOR TAKES OFF GLASSES AT THIS POINT)

Patient: I can't really afford to go private because . . .

Doctor: Let's take a look, shall we? Does that hurt?

Patient: (CRY OF PAIN) Yes.

Doctor: Cancer.

Patient: Oh no.

Doctor: 'Fraid so. Want to go private now?

Patient: Oh God. When will I have to go into hospital?

Doctor: Well, of course, if you want to go in *before* you die, then I'd really recommend private treatment.

Patient: (BREAKS DOWN) I'm sorry. I've no money. I'll have to get it done on the National Health.

Doctor: (DRILY) Very well, as you wish.
(DOCTOR THEN WRITES OUT DEATH CERTIFICATE IN FULL VIEW OF PATIENT)

END OF CONSULTATION.

NOTE: This method of consultation should not be used on infants and young children.

April 28th, 1979

Dear Gamma,

It is becoming evident that Thatcher is going
to win the Election. Enclosed is some
background research culled from various
associates from her early life. I think it
gives a useful insight into her character.

From the Secret Service point of view, she
looks like very good news indeed.

Cheers,

Alpha

P.S. The report card's rather amusing, what?

THATCHER - THE EARLY YEARS

THE YOUNG MARGARET THATCHER, AS OTHERS REMEMBER HER.

Daisy Heslop, a classmate of Margaret's at
Laurel Grove Primary School.

I'll always remember the first time I met Maggie, or
'Snotty' as we used to call her. It was our first
day at primary school, and during the first lesson
the teacher asked us all what we wanted to be.
'Prime Minister' piped up Snotty and we all laughed
and laughed. It doesn't seem quite so funny now.

Jane Williams, another friend at Laurel Grove.

I remember being very impressed with how clever she
was. On one occasion my mother had given me a

packet of liquorice allsorts. I was going to share
them out with all my friends until Maggie explained
that 'in the long-term economic view', as she put it,
it would be better for everyone if she ate the lot.

In no time at all she became the leader of our gang.
She had a jolly nickname for each of us. I remember
mine was 'prole'. What larks we got up to - kicking
away old men's walking sticks, playing 'Cops and
Workers', sending white feathers to Joseph Stalin,
and the most exciting of all, throwing stones at
gypsies. Maggie used to enjoy that. She said we
were doing it out of 'real and justified fears'.
I often see her on TV now, and I think back to those
marvellous days, although I don't watch her as often
as I'd like, because she sets off my husband's
'trouble'.

Mr Boon, formerly maths teacher at Laurel Grove,
now living in Australia.

I remember one day she fell over in the playground
and grazed her knee. She didn't cry, but I could
see her eyes were glazed with tears. I rubbed her
knee comfortingly and said, 'There, there, who's a
brave little girl'. 'Don't touch me', she snapped.
Then she fixed me with a steely glare. 'What's
your name?' she demanded. 'Boon', I replied
hesitantly. 'Boon', she said and noted it down in
her little black book she kept with her. She left
soon after that and I never heard hide nor hair from
her again until I saw her signature at the bottom of
my deportation order.

Miss George, English teacher at Laurel Grove.

She had a very sensitive side to her. I recall she
once wrote an absolutely charming essay entitled
'The Little Girl and the Lamb'. It was all about
this girl who had a pet lamb all of her own. She
loved her lamb very dearly and took it with her
wherever she went. And then one day the lamb grew
up into a lovely big sheep. So she skinned it and
got twenty quid for the carcase.

Mr Trevett, Janitor.

Strange kid. I remember one day she chopped down
the school apple tree. When I asked her why she'd
done it, she said she'd caught it malingering.

Grantham Secondary School
For Girls

Name *Margaret Thatcher*   **SPRING TERM REPORT**   Form *IVC*

Subject			
ENGLISH	D	Poor. Needs to curb her habit of book burning.	SAS
MATHS	C-	Doesn't really understand maths. Has a tendency to copy others' answers.	C.E.
HISTORY	D	DISPLAYS AN UNHEALTHY INTEREST IN ATTILA THE HUN. ALSO INCLINED TO BLAME ALL HISTORICAL REVERSES SINCE 1400 ON THE TOLPUDDLE MARTYRS. OTHERWISE GOOD.	R. Uhm
GEOG.	D-	Must widen her outlook beyond constantly insisting that 'wogs begin at Berwick'.	Sd
LATIN	B+	Good. Strong on imperatives.	HLJ
FRENCH	C-	Her accent reminds me of a ruptured sheep	JJ
PHYSICS	A	Excellent. Works hard. Says she is determined to keep ahead of the Russians.	An.
BIOLOGY	C	Poor. Margaret feels all animals are dirty	B
GAMES	E	Cheats	
R.E.	C	Annoying. Continually misquotes Francis of Assisi and refers to the Good Samaritan as 'that mug'.	HLS

FORM MISTRESS Margaret has the vexing habit of talking while I'm talking and then telling me to stand in the corner. LB.

HEAD MISTRESS Dull but determined. However, should do no lasting damage provided she is kept away from positions of responsibility. AD

Attendance	Appearance
Remorseless.	Metallic.

CALLAGHAN BLASTS THATCHER

From: The Leader of the Opposition

Dear Maggs,

Sorry about that nasty speech yesterday. You know how it is, Benn and Heffer have been on my back again — I'm sure you'll understand.

Anyway, I'm afraid I can't make it for tea tomorrow afternoon. I've got to go and launch some damned Labour campaign to 'sweep you out of office' as they will insist on saying. Not that there's a snowball's chance in hell of <u>that</u> happening, so don't worry.

In any case, Maggs, you know how I feel about the idea of being PM again. The pace of life in Opposition is so much more pleasant; I've been able to spend a lot more time on my farm. The profits from it have fairly shot up, and thanks to your sensible reductions on taxes for the rich, I'm now doing very nicely. What's more, quite frankly I don't much fancy the thought of taking on the miners, the TUC, and the rest of that grubby mob <u>and</u> having to handle 20% inflation. I must say, I admire the way you simply treat the working class like dirt. I think that's what they understand best, don't you? But it's not the kind of idea that goes over big at Labour Party Conferences. (Dearest Maggs, you're the only person I can be really frank with.)

Anyway, I mustn't keep you back from your important job. Sorry about the date for tea. I hope you and Denis will still be able to come round for supper next Saturday. Audrey so looks forward to having 'a bit of class' at the dinner table.

James Callaghan MP

P.S. I may have to ask you a searching question about unemployment in the House next week. They want me to 'denounce you vigorously'. Hope that's OK.

21st March 1980

We now received what was probably Hermes' most spectacular leak so far. At a single stroke there came into our possession a set of documents relating to a hitherto unknown government Propaganda Unit, thought to have been set up by Mrs Thatcher shortly after the 1979 Election. We were completely stunned by the range and subtlety of the government's tactics towards the media.

& Saatchi
Saatchi

Advertising
Consultants

by appointment to the
Prime Minister

4th November 1979

Dear Prime Minister,

We enclose some of the sloganised concepts that
the boys have been running up the flagpole to
see if they flutter. We have also thrown in a
couple of poster ideas that we are rather pleased
with.

Please hit us with a response.

Saatchi
& SAATCHI

P.S. We still think John Biffen is a totally
     unmarketable product.

The Economy

KEEP BRITAIN OUT OF THE RED........
WORK FOR NOTHING.
A Better Britain with the Conservatives.

The EEC

WOGS STILL BEGIN AT CALAIS
Annoy them......
with the Conservatives.

Nuclear Confrontation

HURRAH! HERE COMES THE HOLOCAUST!
Vote Conservative.....
the Party that makes things happen.

Health

PAIN IS JUST YOUR BODY'S WAY
OF TELLING YOU YOU'RE A NHS PATIENT
Go private . . . with the Conservatives.

Race Relations

IF GOD HAD MEANT US ALL TO BE EQUAL,
HE WOULDN'T HAVE INVENTED COLOUR.
The Conservatives . . . . There's none whiter.

Social Security

IS THERE A SCROUNGER IN YOUR STREET?
. . . .Shop him to the Conservatives.

THIS IS ASIF.

He lives in Bangladesh
in total poverty.
He gets hardly any
food to eat....

TOUGH
LUCK
ASIF!

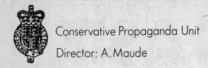

Conservative Propaganda Unit

Director: A. Maude

The Prime Minister	Your reference
10 Downing Street	ANT/MIN
London SW 1	Our reference
	OD/10/UR/ 2
	Date: 21st February 1980

Dear Margaret,

I was intrigued by your proposal that our Propaganda Unit
should fund and launch a magazine for the unemployed.

I have given much thought to this, and firmly believe that
it is a most promising project. I think the essential
thing is to give it a veneer of independence and liberal
thinking while ensuring that in the end it is propagating
the right kind of views ‾ something like the Guardian, in
fact.

I have had a team of writers draw up a few sample pages.
I have also taken the liberty of putting together a sample
page from the new Radio Times, which I believe you plan to
publish directly following next year's absorbtion of the
BBC into the Communications Section of the Home Office.

I think this whole project is very exciting. I hope you
favour the approach as planned at present. I am at your
disposal should you wish to have a talk about it.

Yours sincerely,

Angus

Angus Maude

ENCS

Freetime

A magazine for the unemployed

LIFESTYLE
POLITICS
COOKING
FASHION
ABROAD
TRAVEL

SPECIAL:
PULL-OUT
GUIDE
'Park Benches
Where it's
all at'

Freetime

A magazine for the unemployed

In this week's issue:

Lifestyle:	Anna Raeburn: Gay love on a tight budget. Katharine Whitehorn: Why I hate being rich.
Fashion:	The lean 'n hungry look — why it's here to stay.
Politics:	Jill Tweedle on women Prime Ministers.
Travel:	Tips on making the most of your walk round the block.
Abroad:	Bernard Levin unmasks the scandal of unemployment in the Soviet Union.
Cooking:	Self-denial soup: it's cheap and satisfying PLUS tasty fillings from old newspapers.
AND	All the usual information on what's happening this week on *your* street corner.

WHY I STILL WANT TO SEE A WOMAN IN No. 10

by Jill Tweedle

". . if my child's school *has* to be closed down, I would prefer that it was done by a woman."

I was busy marinating some exquisitely-shaped avocado stones the other evening when the most ghastly noises came echoing out of the attic, where my two teenage sons have made themselves a den. I went in, only to find them engaged in heavy sado-masochism with two local girls whose mothers make rather good wholemeal flans.

It was a difficult situation, the kind that all parents dread.

I chose not to interrupt their fun, but later I took Mark and Adrian aside and explained that while sex could be a viable high-energy experience, nonetheless letting another human being into one's space was about the mutual creation of a committed and ongoing emotional situation. I pointed out that anything which gave two people (or three, or indeed, four people) fulfilment couldn't be wrong, provided they didn't hurt each other. My sons laughed a lot at this, as if I had somehow missed the point.

Afterwards, I got depressed about the whole incident. Where, I wondered, had I gone wrong? God knows, I'd tried for sixteen years to bring up my sons as open-ended ongoing human potentialities, and now here it was all thrown back in my face.

It was then I first thought: thank goodness there's a woman Prime Minister. Certainly, I have in the past taken a stand against some of her policies. I shall continue to do so. But I couldn't help feeling that if my sons' school *has* to be closed down, I would prefer that it was done by a woman. Nobody would pretend that Mrs Thatcher is a force for women's liberation, yet it must surely be of *some* significance that a woman, not a man, is taking the day-to-day decisions that are totally crucial in taking Britain back to the Stone Age. I may not *want* the Stone Age, but I will fight to the death for the right of a woman to take us back to it.

No doubt the lives that my sons

face will not be easy. People will, perhaps, laugh at their imitation leather bikers gear; their future wives may not wish to wear handcuffs in the marriage bed. But if that is the kind of life they have meaningfully chosen, I can only wish them well, and pray that they will find some kind of happiness and fulfilment within their own unorthodox emotional matrix. But would it, I wonder, be entirely wrong of me to hope that the influence of womanhood will slowly begin to permeate this divided nation of ours, until the day comes when men will no longer feel the need to indulge in the sort of sexual expression that has taken my two sons from me? It may, perhaps, be a fond hope, but I'm clinging to it. After all, as I said to myself this morning getting out of the bath: 'Damn it, Jilly, you're a woman. You always were a woman, and you always will be a woman.' And do you know? I felt so much better after that.

Are *you* a woman? If so, Jill Tweedle would like to hear from you. Write and tell her how womanhood has changed your life.

NEXT WEEK:
Jill Tweedle gives some tips on avoiding guilt feelings when travelling in very poor countries.

AUSTER
· A GLI

THE BIN-LINER LOOK
This charming gown consists of two used black bin-liners, sewn together and caught in at the waist with a belt of finest string. (Note: in summer the bottom bin-liner may be detached and used as a functional everyday shopping bag.)

TY FASHIONS

E OF THE VERY LATEST STYLES ·

QUILTED LITTERWEAR
A striking "basse couture" effect, achieved by gluing a wide assortment of litter to a foundation of old sackcloth. Suitable for any occasion (perhaps not the opera).

AND NOW FOR THE MORE DARING . . .
The Topless, Backless, Sideless Evening Belt
Inexpensive and instantly arresting.

FOR HIM . . .

The "Space Look"
Up to date and very, very cool. Just the thing for those long hot summer days lounging around on street corners.

AND FINALLY. . .

The "Peasant Look"
What everyone, but *everyone* will be wearing next year.

SATURDAY tv
BBC 1

9.00 – 12.00
Multi-Coloured Swop Shop

Noel Edmonds invites kids to phone in and shop social security scroungers. Are there any in *your* area?
And, at 10.15: Denis Waterman sings his new hit single: 'Hiving off your Private Parts'. And at 11.20: Sneer with Cheggers. This week Cheggers sneers at very poor people and gives you some smart tips on setting fire to tramps.

12.00
GRANDSTAND

Featuring an outstanding day of sport. Introduced by Harry Carpenter, with special live coverage of *The Freedom Games* from Santiago, Chile. PLUS reports on all the day's main sporting highlights here at home,
including:
12.15: Show jumping
12.50: Polo.
 1.30: Show jumping.
 2.00: Fox hunting.
 2.35: Polo.
 3.05: Show jumping.
 3.20: Live croquet from Wembley.
 4.00: Grouse shooting
 4.15: More show jumping.
(For working class sports: See ITV).

5.45
California Fever

The temperature's rising down at Rick's Place, when a group of young people do their own thing and distribute leaflets advertising Proposition 13.

6.35
What's On Wogan?

—nothing (too expensive).

7.20
Saturday Night at the Movies: Triumph of the Will (rpt)

Sheridan Morley writes: "Watch out for Himmler in a delightful cameo role".

9.15
News (rpt)

9.25
Telford's Change (rpt)

A serial in ten parts by Brian Clarke. Episode eight: Job Satisfaction. Mark begins to feel alive again when he forces the local tobacconist into liquidation.

10.20
Peter Skellern and his Music

With the Clegthorpe Colliery Band. Peter says: "The lads are very enthusiastic; they've lots more time to practise now that the colliery's been closed down."

BBC2

SUNDAY tv
BBC 1

7.40am – 2.45pm
The Open University

Closed till further notice.

2.45
The Sound of Music

(Eighty-third repeat)

5.50
Comedy Classic:
The 1979 Labour Manifesto

6.45
Closedown

Schools Programmes Next Week

Monday:	The Test Card.
Tuesday:	Art: Painting the Test Card.
Wednesday:	A Sideways Look at the Test Card.
Thursday:	German for Schools. Ep 5: Die Testkarte.
Friday:	R.D. Laing: The Test Card and the Self.

9.10
On the Move

This week: M for Means Test.

9.30
Beat the Dole Drums

Isla St Clair visits redundant welders in Sheffield and teaches them the art of crochet.

10.05
The 60:70:80 Show

This week Roy Hudd visits the Brentford Darby & Joan Club and breaks the news that old age pensions have been abolished. Also this week: Some tips from Irene Thomas on making the most of hypothermia.

10.40
Nai Zindagi Naya Jeeva

A magazine for Asian viewers explaining why they ought to go back where they came from.

11.45
Sunday Worship

The Reverend Adrian Stone reads the parable of the talents and explains why God is pro-investment.
Also this week: A Studio Discussion: What should be the response of a committed Christian to the fluctuations of the Green Pound?

12.20
Dallas (eighth repeat)

JR poisons his cat, saws off one of Sue Ellen's legs for a joke, and is appointed head of British Steel.

SUNDAY tv
BBC 1

1.15
It Ain't Half Cheap, Mum

A new comedy series set in the planning department of the BBC.

3.55
Prince Charles – an Appeal

HRH The Prince of Wales appeals for contributions to help all those who, through no fault of their own, happen to be monarchs.

4.25
Pym'll Fix It

David Dalton (9) gets shown around a missile silo. Elizabeth Asher (12) wants to create a new killer bacterium at Porton Down. And Elaine Hartley (15) fulfils her lifelong ambition to obliterate Minsk.

5.30
Petal

The uproarious comedy series based on the life of Percy Petal, the SPG constable with a heart of gold. This week Petal adopts a Pakistani orphan, with hilarious results.

6.05
Points of View

Barry Took simpers over more of your letters and explains the thinking behind the recent sale of Radios 3 and 4 to Rupert Murdoch.

6.20
Closedown

BBC 2

9.10 – 4.30
A Party Political Broadcast by the Conservative Party

(with subtitles for the hard of hearing).

4.30
The Sunday Classic Drama Wuthering Heights

Taxpayer Conscious Theatre Group presents an improvised adaptation of the much-loved book, with amateur actors from the Acres Lane Gilbert and Sullivan Society.

8.30 – 9.00
Life on Earth

A look at workers in their natural environment.

Prog 7: Sir Keith Joseph explores the slums of Glasgow and asks "Why did the evolutionary cycle stop here?"

9.00
Playhouse:
Where Do I Go From Here?

Two old men at a bus stop discuss Einstein's special theory of relativity while they wait for a No 74. (duration: two and a half hours)

11.35
Closedown

Rhodes Boyson reads from 'The Texas Chain Saw Massacre'.

HI SPEED GAS an

announcement

Research has shown that a large number of people are using gas *just because it is cheap*.

In the modern world, we all have to take a more responsible attitude towards the use of precious natural resources. British Gas is playing its part by increasing the price of gas by 245%, starting tomorrow.*

This move will not penalise responsible consumers. What it *will* do is stop the squandering of gas on such wasteful activities as washing the dishes, heating the house and cooking meals.

Join the Gas Misers – Buy a blanket.

Hi Speed Gas – Working for Britain.

*There may have to be a further small adjustment of 150% later in the year.

SCRIPT OF PARTY POLITICAL BROADCAST
To be forwarded to PM's office for final approval.

VOICEOVER:
There now follows a Party Political
Broadcast by the Conservative Party.

GRAMS: 'Land of Hope and Glory' (Elgar).

FILM SEQUENCE:
1. CAPTAIN SCOTT, PLUCKILY MAKING HIS WAY
   THROUGH ANTARCTIC BLIZZARD.

CUT TO: 2. PICKET LINES CHANTING OUTSIDE GRUNWICK.

CUT TO: 3. BATTLE OF BRITAIN PILOTS TAKING OFF TO
   DEFEND BRITAIN.

CUT TO: 4. SCUFFLES AT NOTTING HILL CARNIVAL.

CUT TO: 5. HEROIC EVACUATION OF DUNKIRK.

CUT TO: 6. ENGLISH FOOTBALL FANS RIOTING IN ROME.

CUT TO: 7. PRIME MINISTER SEATED AT DESK.

THATCHER: 'Land of Hope and Glory'. But, you
   know, a lot of people nowadays feel
   that Britain is a place with not much
   hope and precious little glory. (LEAN
   FORWARD HERE.) And the subject that's
   really got them worried is 'Law and
   Order'.

CUT TO: 8. MARCUS FOX, MP, IN FRONT OF STUDIO SET
            OF STREET CORNER.

FOX: And it's on streets like these that they
            get worried. Streets where young
            hoodlums pounce on innocent victims and
            leave them for dead.

            AS HE SPEAKS, AN ACTRESS PLAYING AN OLD
            LADY IS VICIOUSLY BEATEN UP BY THREE
            ACTORS PLAYING SKINHEADS.

CUT TO: 9. NIGEL LAWSON, MP, STANDING AMONG
            FOOTBALL CROWDS HOLDING A GRAPH.

LAWSON: This chart shows the number of old
            ladies who were beaten up under Labour.
            Under this Conservative government such
            assaults have declined rapidly, thanks
            largely to our boosting of police
            strength - plus, of course, a general
            reduction in the number of old ladies.

CUT TO: 10. WILLIE WHITELAW EATING A BIG MAC IN
            'MACDONALD'S'.

WHITELAW: But, you know, we can't do as much as
            we'd like to curb crime, because of lots
            of petty little laws which inhibit the
            police.

CUT TO: 11. MARCUS FOX, MP, ENTHUSIASTICALLY POGOING.

FOX: But what do you, the public, think?

CUT TO: 12. STREET SCENE.

         13. CLOSE-UP OF ACTOR PLAYING DOCKER.

DOCKER: Well, I think the police are
            unnecessarily hampered by having to
            give reasons for arresting people.

         14. CLOSE-UP OF ACTOR PLAYING HOUSEWIFE.

HOUSEWIFE: Suspend Habeas Corpus.

         15. CLOSE-UP OF SAME ACTOR AS PLAYED THE
             DOCKER NOW PLAYING A SHOPKEEPER.

SHOPKEEPER: Introduce 'garotting'. It never did
            Spain any harm.

CUT TO: 16. WILLIE WHITELAW PLAYING TABLE TENNIS
IN WEST INDIAN YOUTH CLUB.

WHITELAW: Those were just a few sensible
suggestions that we'll be looking into.
Because we, as a Party, are committed
to the rule of law.

CUT TO: 17. PRIME MINISTER SITTING IN ARMCHAIR IN
FRONT OF OPEN FIRE IN NO. 10 DOWNING
STREET.

THATCHER: I and my government are absolutely
convinced of the need to bring back to
this country a semblance of law and
order. Believe me (LEAN FORWARD
SINCERELY) when I say that I intend
putting a stop,(NOD EMPHATICALLY) and
I mean a stop (NOD MORE EMPHATICALLY)
to the violence on our streets. (STOP
NODDING, SIT BACK AND RELAX.) You know,
I can't tell you how deeply it
distresses me (FURROW BROWS) that
women and old folk are afraid to walk
the streets. (LEAN CASUALLY ON ARM OF
CHAIR.) What a sad comment on what
happened to this country under Jim
Callaghan. (EXPRESSION OF DISDAIN.)
He did so much to erode the rule of
law (MORE DISDAIN) and hand over power
to the Trade Unions. (OUTRIGHT
DISGUST.) Thankfully, these days are
over. Let there be no doubt in
anyone's mind: lawlessness will not be
tolerated. (FIX CAMERA WITH STEELY
GAZE.)

CUT TO: 18. LORD HAILSHAM OUTSIDE OLD BAILEY

HAILSHAM: Of course, the more criminals we
catch, the more strain it places on
the courts. But we have plans to ease
this problem by encouraging
responsible pleas. That's why we're
currently looking into the possibility
that a plea of 'not guilty' should be
made a criminal offence.

CUT TO: 19. WILLIE WHITELAW PLAYING HOPSCOTCH WITH
             ASIAN CHILDREN.

WHITELAW: But won't that increase prison
             overcrowding? Well, we think we've
             got the answer to that.

CUT TO: 20. WORMSHURST EXPERIMENTAL PRISON.
             GOVERNOR'S OFFICE.

WHITELAW: Here at Wormshurst Experimental we've
(VOICEOVER) been operating a new 'Prisoner
             Relocation Scheme'. Governor John
             Hyde explains.

CUT TO: 21. GOVERNOR HYDE

GOVERNOR HYDE: Well, very simply, under this scheme,
             prisoners are encouraged to contribute
             something positive to society by
             committing suicide.

CUT TO: 22. WIDE SHOT OF PRISON GRAVEYARD

GOVERNOR HYDE: And it's working very well. This
(VOICEOVER) month alone, 24 prisoners have done the
             honourable thing.

CUT TO: 23. PRISONERS GATHERED READING A NOTICE
             BOARD.

GOVERNOR HYDE: Of course, it's a purely voluntary
(VOICEOVER) scheme for the prisoners, but we do
             everything in our power to help the lads
             by depressing them as much as possible.

         24. CLOSE-UP OF NOTICE BOARD SHOWING LONG
             LIST HEADED 'THIS MONTH'S UNFAITHFUL
             WIVES'.

CUT TO: 25. WILLIE WHITELAW IN PUBLIC URINAL

WHITELAW: This move towards 'self-help', plus
             other projects such as prison visits to
             serious offenders by their victims'
             relatives are all aimed at reducing the
             numbers in prison and thus easing the
             burden on the tax-payer.

CUT TO: 26. PRIME MINISTER SEATED AT DESK.

THATCHER: It is positive steps like these which
              show that we mean business. They won't
              solve everything. There are no easy
              answers. (PAUSE OMINOUSLY.) But I am
              determined to restore Britain to its
              former vigour and greatness. I believe
              we can do it. Together. (SIT BACK
              AND SMILE.)

CUT TO: 27. CLOSE-UP OF UNION JACK FLUTTERING IN
             THE WIND.

CAPTION SUPERIMPOSED:

              "Sleep safe in your bed...
               WITH THE CONSERVATIVES."

                    END OF BROADCAST

1st May 1980

This time all we received from 'Hermes'
was a key to a left-luggage locker in
Euston Station. On opening the locker,
we found a green folder. The theme of the
contents was 'surveillance'. The file reveals just
how carefully Mrs Thatcher vetted leading
Conservatives before selecting them for her first
Cabinet. It also points to some of the tensions
behind the scenes as Mrs Thatcher attempts to
track down the prankster in her team. But even
this pales into insignificance alongside the
shattering revelation that the Prime Minister's
surveillance machine extends to the
interception of the Royal Family's private
correspondence.

2nd April 1980

FROM THE OFFICE OF
THE PRIME MINISTER

Sir David McNee
New Scotland Yard
Victoria Street
London SW1

Dear David

Please harass the following:

Arthur Scargill
Paul Foot
Terry Wogan
Jim Prior
Giscard D'Estaing
The Nolan Sisters
Robin Day
The producer of 'Not the Nine O'Clock News'
The producer of 'The Nine O'Clock News'
Kilroy
Keir Hardie (I suspect he's hiding out somewhere)
Nicholas Webb
The population of Newcastle
Emu
The British Olympic Team
Micks
That nancy boy who charged me the full price for
a lampshade in Harrods
and
whoever is responsible for these photographs
(see following pages). Judging by the schoolboy
humour, I'd say this is the work of
St. John-Stevas. Check him out.

M.T.

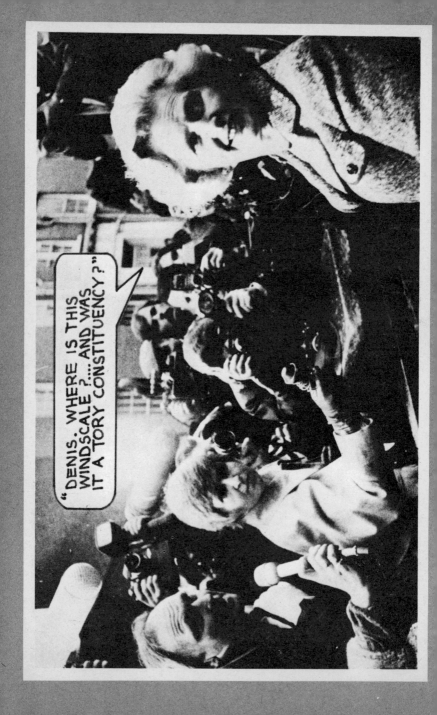

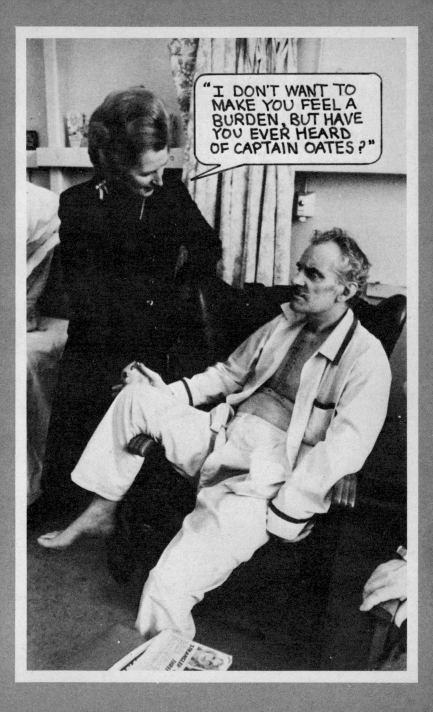

Date as postmark,

The Prime Minister,
10 Downing Street,
London SW1.

Dear Prime Minister,

Here is our report, as requested, on the daily life
of your cabinet colleague 'B'. As you will see, a
substantial degree of wetness has revealed itself.

Should you wish to be rid of this particular individual, I am sure that our Missing Persons Section
would be happy to arrange something. Alternatively,
we would be pleased to submit a quotation for the
arranging of a <u>flagrante</u> <u>delicto</u> situation of your
choosing.

Yours faithfully,

Herbert Graudge

Herbert A. Graudge
Senior Partner,
Graudge & Graundle.

24 HOURS IN THE LIFE OF A WET

From Messrs Graudge & Graundle,
for the attention of the Prime Minister.

STRICTLY PRIVATE

06.48   A light was seen to go on in the main
         bedroom of B's house. Shortly after-
         wards, as suspected, Radio 2 was
         switched on. It was observed that B
         is attracted to the music of Neil
         Sedaka and Des O'Connor, and it has
         been established beyond reasonable
         doubt that B never plays any of the
         Complete Wagner given to him for
         Christmas by the Prime Minister.

07.50   Voices were raised in the house. Our
         long-range microphones were unable to
         pick up the details of the quarrel,
         but shortly afterwards the sound of
         male sobbing was heard coming from
         the main bedroom.

08.32   B emerged from his house. A stray cat
         that had been in the front garden rubbed
         itself against B's legs, and it is
         perhaps of some significance that B did
         not kick the cat out of his way but
         instead bent down and stroked it. B
         then went to his car, which he was

unable to start due to a mechanical
fault. B failed to show any kind of
anger, and set off for the nearest
bus-stop. One of our men remained in
close contact.

08.47   B boarded a No. 24 bus to Whitehall.
He was extremely courteous to the
conductor (a black man) and proceeded
to offer him a 10% tip. (This may, of
course, have been due not to Wetness
but to a lack of experience with public
transport.) As B got off the bus, an
old lady trying to get on remarked that
she had been waiting for a bus for
fifty-five minutes. The conductor was
heard to say 'blame that bitch Thatcher',
and B was seen to chuckle.

09.13   B entered his office. Our hidden video
cameras were able to pick up most of
what followed. B first of all read
the morning papers. These included the
Guardian. It was observed that when he
asked for coffee he said 'please', and
even went so far as to say 'thank you'
in a distinctly friendly tone when the
cup was taken away. At no point during
the morning did B click his heels and
bow in the prescribed manner before the
portrait of the Prime Minister hanging

behind his desk. A report on the
unemployed figures was brought to B
and he failed to look pleased.

11.28   B left his office for lunch with the
        Director-General of the CBI. Several
        lunch-time drinks were consumed. Not
        one of these drinks was goat's blood
        on-the-rocks, as recommended by the
        Prime Minister.

16.35   B returned to his office, where he
        unfortunately hung his coat over our
        video camera.

17.45   B left his office. He proceeded to an
        assignation in an upstairs bar in Soho.
        There he was joined by WET G, who had
        previously informed the Prime Minister
        that he could not join her for the
        Three Million Unemployed Celebrations
        because of 'Prior' (sic) commitments.
        The two Wets were in the bar for almost
        three hours. They were seen to laugh
        frequently, and both had the appearance
        of people who enjoy living. Unsound
        opinions were expressed, including the
        thesis that asphyxiating strikers'
        babies was 'a dodgy idea'.

20.41   Wet B and Wet G were seen to leave the

bar. Wet G excused himself on the
grounds that he 'wanted to get home
and see the kids'. Wet B then proceeded
to Playland, just off Piccadilly Circus,
where he totally ignored the Cosmic
Wars machines and spent instead thirty-
five minutes at the Penny Waterfall,
losing a total of 92 pence.

21.05   B arrived back home.

21.15   B went to bed. Just before doing so,
B was seen to open the front door of
his house, clutching a Paddington Bear
book and dressed in only a long woollen
nightshirt (this was July 17th). He
first put out a saucer of milk for the
cat, then offered a cup of Ovaltine to
the constable on duty outside his home.
B then went back inside, gently closing
the front door.

*Please arrange for Wet B's
name to be publicly associated
with a notorious scandal.
(the Liberal Party?)*

M.T.

FROM THE OFFICE OF
THE PRIME MINISTER

2nd October 1979

Herbert H. Graundle
Senior Partner
Graudge & Graundle,
Private Investigators

Dear Mr. Graundle

I am most grateful to your company for
succeeding in intercepting a number of letters
being exchanged within the Royal Household. I
need hardly tell you that the value of these
letters to me is equalled only by the extreme
confidentiality of all that has been arranged
between myself and your company.

As far as your other proposal is concerned, I do
feel it is rather unfair on Lord Snowdon. Let us
just keep that particular secret under wraps for
the time being. One never knows when it might
come in useful.

Now burn this letter please.

Yours faithfully,

M.T.

Buckingham Palace

24th June. 1979

Dear Charlie,

How are things? Are you having a jolly time
'down under'? I saw a photograph of you yesterday.
You were being kissed by yet another floozie - "Miss
Alice Springs 1980" or something. Do try and dodge
them, dear, if you see them coming. You never
know what you might catch.

Anyway, things are just as bloody here at
Buck H. 'It' came round for its Prime Ministerial
consultation on Thursday, droning on and on
about something to do with Arthur Scargill and
Botany Bay. 'It' also expressed concern over your
Auntie Meg's shenanigans with the Llewellyn person.
'It' suggested I put something in Meg's tea. I ask
you! As if we hadn't tried that.

Your father goes quite barmy every time 'It'
arrives. He locks himself in his study and
punches the wall. He says Thatcher addresses
him like a public convenience. 'It' also has
an unfortunate effect on the Corgis' digestion.

Roll on the return of that Callaghan person.
He may have been a bit rude, and he stonked
like Quasimodo, but at least he didn't keep
asking if he could borrow my imperial mace.

Love,
Mum

Wolamaloo Surf Club
New South Wales Australia

1st July 1979

Dear Mater,

Ying tong ying tong ying tong ying tong ying tong iddle I po! My knees pinged with pleasure on receiving your letter. This has to be a short letter as I've to go out in a minute to be photographed falling over and laughing.

I know what you mean about the Thatcher person. She's a real cold fish. I'll never forget when I introduced her to the Three Degrees and she asked to see their entry permits. Just think, back in the good old days we could have had her head lopped off. Still, keep your chin up, she's only in for another four years. (Joke, joke).

Your ever loving

Charlie

P.S. I got a joke dogturd through the post yesterday. I assume this was from Anne's Mark

P.P.S. You dirty rotten swine, you deaded me.

Buckingham Palace

24th June. 1979

Dear Anne.

How are things with you? An exploding cucumber arrived in the post today. I presume Mark was responsible. Do ask him to stop, dear. One of the equerries nearly lost a hand.

Things are as bad here as ever. It is driving me bonkers. She keeps trying to get me to dissolve Parliament and declare martial law, just because some local council is refusing to demolish its libraries. I can't take much more.

Halfway through yesterday's consultations. Sam. my favourite Corgi. upped and bit Thatcher. Most upsetting. The vet says Sam won't last the night.

Love.

Mum

HRH Princess Anne
Gatscombe Park
Buckinghamshire

14th September 1979

Mother,

Got your letter. Know what you mean about Thatcher. She still refuses to grant the increase in my allowance which is essential if I am to extend the stables into Warwickshire. If I was you, I'd tell her to sod off.

Anne.

PS: Sorry about the exploding cucumber. Have sent Mark to bed without his supper.

Subject: Sir Geoffrey Howe

Born: 1926

Educated: Winchester & Trinity Coll. Cambridge.

The subject admires the philosophies of Adam Smith, John Stuart Mill, Rolf Harris, and Larry the Lamb. Known affectionately to his friends as 'Mogadon'. Possesses a practical intelligence: brilliantly adept at joined-up writing and tying his shoelaces. Deep Tory principles come from having been bitten in his pram by a coalminer.

Interests:	None.
Ambition:	To be loved.
Hobbies:	Warm Ribena drinking and sitting still.
Weaknesses:	Tells the truth sometimes.
Statements worth noting:	"Money can't buy you happiness. But then happiness isn't everything, is it ?"
Assessment:	Reliable, subservient, dull. Good Cabinet material.

Subject: Patrick Jenkin.

Born: 1926

Educated: Dragon School, Oxford, Clifton College & Jesus Coll. Cambridge.

674102

Solid, if unspectacular, hardliner. Rationaliser. Bright ideas include introducing the rack as an alternative to Social Security claims. Thinks Sparta was the perfect welfare state. Member of Heath's government (70-74) when he advised nation to save energy by brushing their teeth in the dark. But thought to be "not mad in the conventional sense". Always wears striped shirts to tell him which way up he is.

Interests:	Rats. Thalidomide.
Ambition:	To close down the world.
Hobbies:	Adventure holidays in Chile, motorway accidents, and setting fire to tramps.
Weaknesses:	Suspected of liking Ted Heath.
Statements worth noting:	None.
Assessment:	Malleable. Interest in Sparta suggests he would make ideal Minister for Social Security.

Subject: Norman St. John-Stevas.

Born: 1929

Educated: Ratcliffe College,
Fitzwilliam Coll.
Cambridge & Christchurch
Coll. Oxford.

235647

Thrown out of school at the age of twelve for taking
baths in asses' milk after rugger matches. Only
member of the Party who waxes his underwear. Known
as 'the thinking man's Frankie Howerd', he can be
spontaneously witty if given three days warning.
Models himself on the Albert Memorial, and was
converted to the Catholic Church because they have
dinkier vestments. Likes opera because it's under-
stated. A great benefactor of the arts, he once
played the handbag in 'The Importance of Being
Earnest'. Known to his friends as 'Dioxin'.

Interests:	Orifices.
Ambition:	Immortality.
Hobbies:	Talking loudly at parties.
Weaknesses:	Big mouth.
Statements worth noting:	"Pretentious, moi ?".
Assessment:	A good crawler, but basically unsound. Might be useful in some kind of meaningless cosmetic post. Suggest Minister for the Arts.

Subject: William Whitelaw.

Born: 1918

Educated: Winchester & Trinity Coll.
Cambridge.

815436

A popular figure. Jovial, uncle-type. Has been known
to display liberal humanitarian principles, but only
when convenient. A firm supporter of strong law and
order policies, he believes in short, sharp
sentences, such as "Cripes!" and "Gosh, I'm Chubby".
Plays the oaf to avoid awkward questions.

Interests:	Niceness through the ages.
Ambition:	To be reincarnated as a labrador.
Hobbies:	Putting on weight.
Weaknesses:	Tends to dribble in public.
Statements worth noting:	"I like everybody".
Assessment:	Benign exterior makes him the right person to announce unpleasant measures. Possible Home Secretary.

Subject: Lord Carrington

Born: 1919

Educated: Eton College & RMC Sandhurst.

480617

Proud of his aristocratic connections. As a child was considered deformed because he had a chin. Owing to his great inherited wealth was originally christened 'No. 2 Account' (later changed by deed poll). An industrious and ambitious man, he started at the top and worked his way across. Very dignified. Thinks smiling is vulgar. Only goes to the toilet on special occasions. Believes in government through condescension. As Minister of Defence under Heath he campaigned for NATO forces to be better dressed.

Interests:	Heriditary diseases.
Ambition:	To bring back forelocks.
Hobbies:	Deportment, reciting Burke's Peerage.
Weaknesses:	Outmoded sense of humour.
Statements worth noting:	"Behind every grey man there's a great woman".
Assessment:	Distant air would make him a good Foreign Secretary. Might be the right man to supervise transition to Rhodesian independence, though cannot be relied upon to rig elections properly.

Subject: Sir Keith Joseph

Born: 1918

Educated: Harrow & Magdalen Coll.
Oxford.

The subject is undoubtedly one of the Party's leading
thinkers. A man of many ideas, most of them Milton
Friedman's. Acquired considerable management
experience at Bovis as Chief Tea-trolley Executive
(1951-55), later promoted to Litter Disposal
Consultant (1955-61). Published works include
'Monetarism in the Late Renaissance', 'The Sub-
Divided Self' and 'Why I believe in Flying Saucers'.

Interests: Psychic phenomena. The Thirties.

Ambition: To walk from Westminster to
Putney without stepping on the
cracks.

Hobbies: Poisoning goldfish, talking to
plants, and "just pottering about
in the toilet".

Weaknesses: See separate file.

Statements "Wollt Ihr den totalen Krieg?".
worth noting:

Assessment: Persecution complex suggests he
would make a good hatchet man.

Subject: Dr Gerard Vaughan.

Born: 1923

Educated: Privately, in East Africa.
Later University of London.

Medically qualified. Once lost 614 patients in one day. Believes hospitals would be more efficient if they ceased to exist. A radical diagnostician, he won acclaim for his medical thesis arguing that death is a form of advanced hypochondria. Also dismisses Rabies as "psychosomatic".

Interests:	Pain
Ambition:	To operate on Arthur Scargill.
Hobbies:	Pulling the legs off spiders. Sneering.
Weaknesses:	When he attempts to smile bears frightening resemblance to vampire.
Statements worth noting:	None.
Assessment:	Seems the obvious choice to put the NHS to sleep.

BRITISH BROADCASTING CORPORATION

TELEVISION CENTRE WOOD LANE LONDON W12 7RJ

TELEPHONE 01-743 8000 TELEX: 265781

TELEGRAMS AND CABLES TELECASTS LONDON TELEX

MEMORANDUM

From: The Director General of the BBC

To: The Prime Minister

My dear Mrs Thatcher,

Here, as requested, is a transcript of tonight's news
bulletin on BBC1. As you are aware, we at the BBC place
great stress upon our editorial independence. However,
if there's anything you don't like, we'll change it. I
would be grateful if you could return the amended script
by 8.30 this evening at the latest.

Please do not forget to let me have your monthly list of
which producers to sack.

With regard to the question of the offensive joke about
Sir Keith Joseph and the brass monkey, broadcast in last
week's Basil Brush Show, I have taken the severest measures;
the producer in question has now been appointed sports
correspondent in Afghanistan.

Do please give my regards to Denis, and thank him for his
note. I am so glad that he enjoys Playschool.

With deepest affection and highest esteem,

Ian Trethowan

Ian Trethowan
DG BBC

P.S. We have given considerable thought to your idea
about a change of name for the BBC, but some of
my colleagues still feel that 'Conservative Central
Office' might lay itself open to attack from Left-
wing elements. What Do you think ?

BBC NINE O'CLOCK NEWS BULLETIN

Thursday April 12th 1980

NEWSREADER:

Good evening. The latest unemployment
figures reveal that there has been an
encouraging downturn in the overall upturn
in the out of work. For the second month
running, the number of unemployed is less
than the population of Norway. A
government spokesman described the figures
as 'hopeful' and pointed out that one
person in four is now unemployed, compared
with one person in three who is a heavy
smoker. However, a Labour Party spokesman
described the latest figures as 'outrageous'.

*and said it was nothing to what labour
could do if they were back in power.*

*I've added
a line or
two here →
M.T.*

Education. Another twenty-three schools
in the Birmingham area are to be closed
as part of a programme of rationalisation.
Mrs E Gidhart Ewing, a teacher in Bear Creek,
Wisconsin, described the decision as
'courageous'.

*please
note*

Small

Defence. This afternoon there was a
demonstration in Trafalgar Square against
the proposed deployment of Cruise missiles
on Hampstead Heath. Protesters waving
banners marked 'No Cruise missiles' were
arrested and charged with being in possession
of offensive weapons.

*It must
have been
tiny
M.T.*

The disabled. This afternoon, Mr Reg Prentice,
Minister for the Disabled, opened the new
Lord Palmerston Centre for the Limbless.

V. good.

Based upon a new self-help principle, the
Centre is funded by raffles and bring-and-buy
sales. Mr Prentice chatted to inmates and
shook artificial limbs with them. Mr Prentice
then made a short informal speech, in which he
pointed out that giving people wheelchairs only
bred an unhealthy dependence upon the state.
He looked forward to the time when all disabled
people would once again be given the independence
and dignity of fending for themselves and
building their own artificial limbs.

Isn't Reg a blessing!

Foreign News

Northern Ireland. Early this morning in the
Falls Road area of Belfast two ~~teenagers~~ IRA men were
shot dead by troops when they failed to stop
at a road block. They were rushed to hospital,
but were found to be dead on arrival. No names
have yet been released. ← *Why not?!*

And we've just heard that ~~a car bomb has~~
exploded in a village in County Antrim, killing
seventeen people ~~and~~ injuring eleven others.
Several ~~shops~~ and more than eight houses were
flattened by the blast. No organisation has
~~yet claimed responsibility.~~

there has been a small earthquake in Northern Perry in which two people and a llama have lost their lives

INSERT HERE M.J

And finally, a heart-warming story from
Newcastle. Emily Soskind, a five-year-old
who suffers from multiple sclerosis, was given
a puppy dog for her birthday. She decided to
call him 'Floppy'. But Floppy ran away, and
after three months of searching, Emily's family
feared that the dog would never be seen again.
Emily was heartbroken. Until, that is,
yesterday, when Emily and her family went on a
day trip to Boulogne and there was Floppy
standing on the quayside wagging his tail.

No. Shushy

Floppy and Emily are now happily re-united...
Sounds like a case of 'dogged determination'.
Goodnight.

who writes this stuff SEE ME M.J.

On this occasion the package from 'Hermes' was accompanied by 24 red roses. This raised the obvious question: was Hermes' secret life placing him under considerable mental stress? Certainly he was becoming increasingly bold. Given the intimate nature of the documents, it is difficult to see how he could possibly have obtained them without gaining access to the Prime Minister's personal belongings.

14 February. 1949

1 The Ramblings
Eastbourne.

Dearest Margaret,

I am writing this to you because I know that if I tried to tell you to your face I would only stammer and you would call me a 'cretinous oaf' like you did last night.

But there is no denying that your takeover of my senses has started a spate of speculative activity in my heart, and only an executive statement from you can restore stability to my emotional market.

Enclosed is a love poem. (Could I have a receipt, please?)

All my confidence

Denis

TO MY MARGARET

This little city heart of mine's
To overflowing full,
The market may be bear, my love,
But I feel like a bull.

Let's speculate together, love,
Let's build our love on rock,
Within your site allow me to
Erect my tower block.

And when life's shades are closing in,
When you and I are old, love,
We'll both retire to Switzerland
And speculate in gold, love.

14, Ben Jonson Crescent,
Woodstock.

27th February, 1949

Dear Mr Thatcher,

I am in receipt of your love letter of
the 14th inst.

I do not recall invoicing a love poem
from you. I suggest you check your
records.

Yours faithfully,

Margaret Roberts

LETTER
MISSING
HERE

HERMES

14, Ben Jonson Cresent,
Woodstock.

9th April, 1949

Dear Denis,

Re: Your birthday present.

I acknowledge receipt of your esteemed
gift. Thank you. I have tried it on,
but it left nasty bruises.

Please watch your margins.

Margaret

1 The Ramblings
Eastbourne

3rd June 1949

My darling ~~Margaret~~ Buster,
   I am sorry about last night, I really am. I feel particularly guilty about the carpet. I do hope it hasn't stained. Can you ever forgive me?

Contritely
Denis

14, Ben Jonson Crescent,
Woodstock.

6th June, 1949

Dear Denis,

I feel it is time for a statement on policy. I like your company. Indeed, I like all your companies. I like the refined and intelligent conversation we have together, the way we have a common interest in the finer points of life, such as money, the status quo, and backgammon. But please understand that I will not put up with all this sticky gooey business that all men seem so fascinated with.

If the day should come when we are married, then I shall consider it my duty to permit an assault upon my orifices. Until such time, I feel we must contain our physical liaison to the familiar goodnight peck on the cheek, which I have always found both proper and stimulating.

With all due affection,

Margaret

My darling Margaret,
   Will you Marry Me?

      Yours breathlessly
         Denis

Dear Denis,

No.

      Margaret

My dearest heart,
   PLEASE will you Marry Me?

      Yours on the window ledge
         Denis

Dear Denis,

   NO.

      Margaret

Light of My Life
   Please, please, Marry Me, I beg you.

      Yours absolutely frantically
         Denis

Dear Denis,

Oh, all right then.

Margaret
P.S. Now stop writing these letters.

This book belongs to…

Margaret Thatcher

My Poetry Book

Cows

Of all God's simple creatures
It's cows I really like.
Cows never go on demos,
Cows never go on strike,
Cows never go out picketing,
Cows never make a fuss,
Cows never feel they have the right
To have a local bus.
Cows don't belong to unions
And cows are overjoyed
To lie upon a hillside
Entirely unemployed.
Cows don't require much housing,
A simple shed will do,
Cows never mind if they get milked
Or chopped up for a stew.

Moral . . .

Despite the problems that we face,
This land could be a lovely place,
If only people could be trained
To live like cows and not complain.

My Career – A sonnet

I still remember how my time was spent
In shopping, cooking and in keeping house;
My sole ambition was to be content
With being just another lonely spouse.
Then I was hit by women's liberation
And realised this way of life must stop;
I wrote my name above my female station
And carved a lonely pathway to the top.
They called me iron maiden, shrew and hen,
They never thought that I would make the grade;
But now that I am dominating men
Dear sisters, please don't think you've got it made:
I'm not so women's-libby as you think,
I want all *other* women slaving at the sink.

The Old Missile Base, Grantchester.

Just outside my little room
The missile base begins to loom,
And now there's nothing left to lose
Let's sit and watch the missiles cruise.
I packed my bag and took a train
And got me to England once again,
For England's the one land I know
Where men with nuclear bombs may go.
And Berkshire – loveliest of shires,
The place for bombs on rubber tyres,
And of that district I prefer

The ones that offer nuclear power.
Let other nations waste their breath,
Give me an *English* megadeath.
And may God grant what I should like:
An English first pre-emptive strike.
For Russian people rarely smile
Being communist and packed with guile.
But English people love their land
And don't want nuclear missiles banned,
And when they get to feeling old
They up and start a war I'm told.
Say. . .
Stands the church clock at ten to three,
And is there still some time for tea?

My Family

Families are wonderful,
Though quite a worry too;
Sometimes they so embarrass me
I can't think *what* to do.

Denis never looks at me,
And Carol likes MPs,
Mark's been known to take a fee
For wearing dungarees.

All children are like voters,
Their whining never stops,
The best thing one can give them is
A slap across the chops.

Old Folks

I always like the old folks,
They're kind and nice and sweet.
But they *will* keep on insisting
On having food to eat.

They seem to think that pensions
Can simply grow on trees,
They won't accept their duty is
To sit at home and freeze.

When will they stop complaining?
Why don't they stay in bed?
They've not got much to moan about—
God knows, they'll soon be dead.

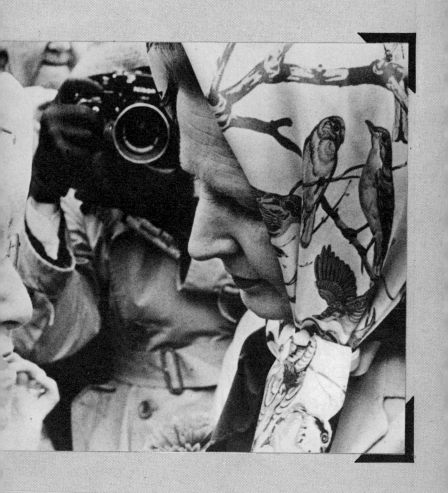

Troops Out of Ireland

I do not know how often
In these dark and dreadful days
My thoughts have turned to Ireland
And those dreadful Irish ways.

To those who think they're winning
By the rifle and the bomb,
I promise you that one day soon
I'll bring the troops back home.

But they won't be sent to Germany,
The Middle East, or France,
My soldier boys in British towns
Will dance a Tory dance.

In Birmingham and Glasgow,
In London and in Leeds,
I'll put the troops out on the streets
—It's troops that Britain needs.

With squaddies on the corner
And bren-guns in the park,
I'll make the streets of Britain safe
To die in after dark.

Professor Milton Friedman,
1478 Fifth Avenue,
New York City.

TO: Mrs Thatcher,
    10 Downing Street,
    London,   16 May 1980
    England.

My dear Margaret,

Well, here I am back home in the States,
where I must say I get nowhere near as much
attention as I do in your dear little
country. It would be lovely to meet again
soon. You might think of arranging another
international symposium on inflation.

I am currently trying to con the BBC into
letting me do another series for them.
This one would be entitled 'Why a return to
the Stone Age makes economic sense'.

I hear some jealous individuals in the
media and on your own backbenches are
trying to turn you against me. Don't listen
to them. When I hear that you are closing
down five more shipyards and sacking
another 60,000 civil servants, it simply
brings tears to my eyes. To think that you
would do all that just for me.

I feel our friendship is strong and endur-
ing. Do not let an increase in the money
supply ever some between us.

Love
Milton Friedman

21st May 1980

Professor Milton Friedman
1478 Fifth Avenue,
New York City.

My dear Milt

There need never be any doubt that our friendship will endure.

I think you might be interested to know that I'm
going to slash public spending by another 35%.
Also, to help control the money supply, I am
going to ban shopping (except for those earning
above £15,000 P.A.). I hope you approve.

I'm afraid this letter must be short and sweet,
as Heseltine is due in for one of his
consultative fawns. Sir Keith sends you his
love; he says he's very well and so is his
giraffe.

I'll be seeing you soon no doubt. If the BBC has
the temerity to refuse your idea for a series, I
shall send the whole outfit to the knackers' yard.

love
Margaret

P.S. Sir Keith has suggested sending kids
     up chimneys. Would this constitute
     'intervention'?

3rd September 1980

O n this date a butcher's boy delivered a 7lb frozen turkey. On close examination, we discovered that alongside the giblets there nestled a tightly-rolled bundle of documents wrapped in polythene. This time 'Hermes' had sent us a sort of lucky dip of information, so varied as to defy categorisation.

Meeting of Special Cabinet Committee M.I.S.C. 7
on Tuesday 8th July 1980.

Subject: <u>The Purchase of the Trident Missile System</u>

Present: Rt Hon Margaret Thatcher, MP.
        Rt Hon William Whitelaw, CH, MC, MP.
        Rt Hon Francis Pym, MC, MP.
        Rt Hon The Lord Carrington, KCMG, MC.
        Rt Hon Sir Geoffrey Howe, QC, MP.

Classified Security

NB: The minutes of this meeting come under
Special Security Classification 2A.
ie:
Nobody other than the above-named persons
may have access to the minutes of this
meeting or to any classified information
relating to this meeting or to any
decision under discussion by the above
persons other than decisions already
reached and published.

In particular, <u>no word of this meeting
must be allowed to reach the Overseas and
Defence Committee of the Cabinet</u>.

The Prime Minister began by describing the
available options, which she wanted discussed
fully and frankly before coming to a collective
decision. These options she described as:

a) The purchase of the Trident missile system

   OR

b) The purchase of the Trident missile system.

The Chancellor of the Exchequer pointed out that
Trident would cost approximately £5,000,000,000
(at 1978 prices) over the next fifteen years, plus
a further £600,000,000 if a fifth submarine was
later added. He argued that this was the wrong way
to dispose of vast sums of money which could be
more usefully given away in tax concessions to
the very rich.

The Prime Minister agreed on the need for protect-
ing the investing classes, but argued that the sum
of five to six billion pounds could easily be saved
by cutting back on wasteful and utopian schemes
like education.

The Home Secretary suggested that the Prime
Minister had got her priorities all wrong. The
Prime Minister suggested that the Home Secretary
button his lip.

The Defence Secretary was asked by the Foreign
Secretary to give to the meeting details of
the strike power of the Trident system, together
with an exact description of proposed deployment
arrangements. The Defence Secretary replied and
explained that the missiles would be 'jolly

powerful' and would be kept underwater to stop
them exploding during heatwaves.

The Prime Minister was enthusiastic about the idea
of keeping missiles underwater. She argued that
this was an excellent way of keeping demonstrators
away from missile bases. Was there any large
stretch of water in Suffolk, asked the Prime
Minister, which could be used for storing the
Cruise missile system? The Home Secretary knew
of a boating lake in Thorpeness but didn't think
it would be big enough for the job. The Defence
Secretary proposed keeping demonstrators under
water, and the Home Secretary promised to report
back on the feasibility of such a scheme.

The Chancellor of the Exchequer continued to press
the Prime Minister for assurances that the nation
could really afford the large sums of money
involved in the purchase of the Trident system.
The Prime Minister said nothing in reply, but
stared at the Chancellor for several seconds
before writing something down in a small black
notebook.

The Prime Minister concluded the discussion by
summing up the arguments for and against the
Trident system. She asked everyone present to
examine their consciences carefully before
voting Yes.

The result of the voting was:

For the Trident system: 5 votes.
Against the Trident system: No votes.

The Prime Minister closed the meeting immediately,
as she was due to chair that afternoon's session
of the All-Party Committee on the Harassment of
Ex-Olympic Competitors.

PARLIAMENTARY ANSWER BY SIR GEOFFREY HOWE

(FIRST DRAFT)

In reply to the Rt Hon Gentleman's question, the intention of the Government in pursuing a monetarist policy can be summed up simply as follows:

In order to contain inflation, money must be made expensive. This is achieved by the maintenance of high interest rates. High interest rates attract important foreign investment. This inflow of foreign money helps to maintain a strong Pound. The consequent high level of the Pound increases the cost of British exports. This leads to a reduction in the amount of British goods exported and thus the closure of unviable factories. The closure of unviable factories increases unemployment. Increased unemployment leads to lower wage claims. Lower wages mean a reduced national buying power. A reduced national buying power from viable factories means the closure of most of British industry. This means an increased level of expensive foreign imports, thereby fuelling inflation.

In order to contain inflation, money must be made expensive. This is achieved by the maintenance of high interest rates. High interest rates attract important...

CONTINUE HERE AND REPEAT TILL END OF QUESTION TIME

MAGGIE HAVE I GOT THIS RIGHT? Geoffrey

11 December 1979   Sir Keith Joseph,
                                   'Elba',
                                   Weybridge.

Dear Maggie,

    While conversing with my rhododendrons
    yesterday I struck on a brilliant idea,
    which I have loosely outlined in the
    attached article. William Deedes has
    promised that The Telegraph will publish
    it as an editorial. Must dash, as I'm
    feeling dizzy. Trust no one.

                        Yours,

                             K.

THE ANCIENT ROOTS OF THE RELIGION OF MONETARISM

Monetarism, as we all know, has been the basis for all the great civilisations that have graced this planet Earth. The ancient Minoans on Crete were ardent monetarists and Sir Arthur Evans' excavations in 1916 revealed conclusively that the palace at Knossos was financed entirely by private enterprise. Troy, too, flourished under Monetarism and many historians believe that the legendary wooden horse, which proved the Trojans' destruction, is an allegory for massive public spending. Similarly the Roman Empire blossomed under Monetarist belief and did not begin to fall until the Emperor Justinian started printing 'confetti dinarii' in 411 A.D.

The Pharaohs, we know, were also fervent monetarists who used to keep their millions of unemployed busy by building pyramids. So Monetarism is not a new civilising influence, it has been with us since the Flood. (A Hebrew parable, incidentally, illustrating the importance of making across-the-board cuts.)

But these are the mere outward trappings of Monetarism; what of its inner mystical truth? This is something we know very little about. We do know, however, thanks to the studies of Professor Hayek, that the Minoan monetarists (circa 2000 B.C.) laid great emphasis on the supernatural. Evidence suggests that they worshipped the number ten and believed that by constantly cutting everything by 10% the whole world could eventually be whittled away to nothing, and thereby achieve a state of purity. An inscription found on a stone tablet at Phaestus in Crete reads: ∧\/⅃⊃⟨ ⊂ᐸ~〜ノ⊔⅄⅃⊃⌐⌐

This, loosely translated, means:
"One in ten,
Cut one in ten,
Then cut one in ten again.
All things be by tenths bereft,
Till, by tenths, there's nothing left."

This devotional verse gives us a considerable insight into the intensity of their belief and also helps explain why the Minoan civilisation disappeared.

The Roman creed of Monetarism brought with it a sacrificial
element. From accounts in Livy, we know the Roman people
used to assemble at the Temple to Apollo who, as well as the
God of Art and Beauty, was also the God of Money Supply.
At the altar, a live duck would be covered in exotic
unctions before having its legs smashed by a ceremonial
club. The High Priest would then raise the duck heaven-
wards and cry "Ecce! Anas clauda non digna vitae."
(Translation: Behold, one lame duck not worthy of life.)
The High Priest would then wring the duck's neck and file
it under "non capax contendere" (non-competitive).

The examples of Monetarist ritual continue through many
cultures down through the ages. The Ottoman massacre of
9,000 Christians in Istanbul in 1311 is now widely held
among scholars to have been a government plan to save on
Social Security benefits. (Ditto Herod's controversial
decision to kill all first-born.) The casual and surprised
poses of the bodies entombed in volcanic ash at Pompeii
indicate a strong non-interventionist line by the author-
ities. Attila the Hun, a strong believer in "less government", was converted to Monetarism as a child, as was
Genghis Khan. And the battle-cry of the Vikings, perhaps
the greatest monetarists of all, was "Elsk Vorduth Sven
Slo", ancient Norse for "No U-Turns".

So why then did Monetarism fade away, until its present
revival? The growth of Christianity, with its expensive
emphasis on responsibility towards the community, seems to
have been partly to blame. (The New Testament, in particular, totally ignores the problems of the wages spiral.)

The increasing awareness of the lower socio-economic classes
(attributable largely to the damaging work of William
Caxton) resulted in a proliferation of non-economical
philosophies which revolved around spurious concepts of
equity and justice. The barrenness of these concepts has
now, happily, been thoroughly exposed, enabling a speedy
return to the rock-solid values of the ancient ways.

The decline of serious Monetarist belief in our society has
bred despair and anarchy. Now it is time to create a new
Radicalism based on tradition. It is time to restore the
old gods. Only by looking backwards, can we go forward.

Dr Gerard Vaughan (M.R.C.V.S.)
MINISTRY OF HEALTH
Whitehall.

The Prime Minister   4 July 1980
10 Downing Street,
London. SW1.

Dear Margaret

Enclosed as requested the draft of a public
information booklet, designed to ease the
burden on the National Health Service.

Yours Ever

Gerard

P.S. Hope Denis' trouble is better.

D-I-Y N.H.S.

If you are unable to wait for a consultation under the NHS, and don't have the sense to go private, here are some useful operations that you can have at home.

APPENDIX

A. The Appendectomy
If your appendix is hurting, this is what to do:–

1. Lie down on a table (preferably covered with a clean tablecloth).

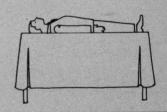

2. Take a sharp knife and make an incision.

3. Remove appendix and throw it away.

Turn over.

4. Get up and go to work.

B. The Lobotomy
If you worry needlessly about the
state of the country and are prone
to futile bouts of depression, this
is what you do.

1. Detach forehead.(Don't throw
it away, you'll need it later.)

2. Cut frontal lobe.

3.Replace forehead and go to
work.

NOTE: Do not be concerned if
you are suffused with a general
sense of well-being and
indifference.

C. Kidney Transplant

If you think you need new kidneys and you don't want to wait 36 years, here is what you do:–

1. Kill someone, first ensuring that they have healthy kidneys. (Warning: some people lie about the state of their kidneys.)

2. Take the kidneys out.

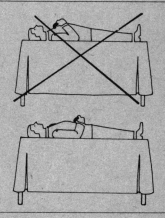

3. Perform stages 1) and 2) of 'Appendectomy'. Then stuff the kidneys into your own body. *Make sure they are in the right place.*

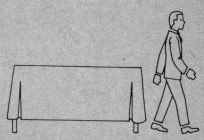

4. Get up and go to work.

22nd October 1980

Another buff envelope. With it was enclosed a solitary sheet of paper bearing the words:
"You may not be hearing from me for some time. —Hermes."
However, Hermes' parting shot was to provide us with yet another sensational disclosure.

PROTECT AND SURVIVE

Procedures to be followed by the public in the event of hostilities breaking out between Her Majesty's Government and enemy Labour Councils

PHASE 1: THE BUILD-UP

Any confrontation will be signalled by a period of mounting tension. This phase will be characterised by unprovoked acts of aggression by the enemy powers. These may include:–

a) Demands for Lebensraum from Lambeth council.

b) The violation of agreed expenditure borders.

c) The council annexation of private schools.

d) Skirmishes between government peace-keeping forces (the SPG) and guerrilla meals-on-wheels vans.

e) The mobilisation of reservist ancillary workers.

f) The storming of Conservative Association offices with a view to taking the occupants hostage until Patrick Jenkin is handed over for trial.

g) General cussedness from council bolshies.

During this phase there is nothing the public can do, except keep calm and don't panic. Simply keep your family indoors, hold hands, and reminisce about the 1960s.

PHASE 2: DEFENSIVE MEASURES

During this phase the Government will attempt to contain the conflict by a series of controlled defensive measures. These may include:–

a) A funds blockade, designed to starve the enemy into bankruptcy.

b) The deployment of ground-to-ground surface generalisations.

c) The conscription of the silent majority.

d) The activation of Lord Denning.

e) A televised speech by Michael Heseltine asking 'who runs the country?' (Note: after this, a full-scale confrontation will be considered inevitable.)

Again, there is little you can do during this phase. Try taking up macramé.

PHASE 3: PREPARE AND PROTECT

At the point when conflict becomes imminent (see Phase 2,e.) ALL PUBLIC SERVICES WILL CEASE TO EXIST. Therefore you must do the following to ensure the safety of you and your family.

i) **Stock up with enough food (where available) for three years* of unparalleled austerity.**

ii) **Build a shelter at the bottom of your garden.** This will come in useful when your house is knocked down to make way for a free enterprise zone. (Note: if your house does not have a garden, it serves you right for being a low earner.)

iii) **Guard against hypothermia.** Wrap granny in baco-foil. (Note: if you are threatened by starvation, simply roast her in a moderate oven, basting at regular intervals.)

*Longer, if we get re-elected.

iv)   **Whitewash all windows.** This won't protect you, but it will stop you looking out of the window and getting depressed by what you see.

PHASE 4: DESPAIR AND DUCK

The full-scale conflict will take many forms. These will require separate defensive responses.

i)   All NHS hospitals will be strafed by the RAF, so **you must evacuate any hospitalised relatives to a place of safety.** (eg: a private clinic, Harrods, a lime pit.)

ii) Defoliants will be deployed on municipal parks and gardens, so **whatever you do, don't do it behind a bush.** (Note: there may be some napalming of adventure playgrounds, so be prepared: check that your children are insured against fire.)

iii) The neutron bomb will be dropped on any boroughs sympathetic to the enemy. This weapon depopulates inner-city areas but leaves property intact*. Therefore take the necessary measures now:
Get your money into property.

*Based on an idea by Wandsworth Housing Committee.

PHASE 5: THE AFTERMATH

Subsequent to the cessation of hostilities, you may encounter some minor difficulties. These may include:–

a)   The absence of roads, hospitals, sewers, transport and other luxuries.

b)   A new penal code, which will include amputation, flogging and decapitation for 'crimes against monetarism'.

c)   Big holes in the ground.

REMEMBER!
The biggest danger is contamination from lethal levels of rationalisation. Tell-tale signs of rationalisation include a shrinking of vital wages, rapid loss of job, and being boiled down for glue.

REMEMBER!
These will be troubled times, so if you want to survive:–

  i) Do not wear 'Don't blame me, I voted Labour' badges.
 ii) Do not share food.
iii) Do not look surplus to requirements.

REMEMBER!
There is one way that you and your family can be sure of surviving the coming confrontation:
Move to a Conservative-controlled borough.

Who is 'Hermes'? A top-ranking civil servant? A trusted Parliamentary Private Secretary? A relative of Mrs Thatcher? Or even a member of the Cabinet? Is he still at large? Or has he perhaps been detected? These are the questions that are bound to be raised.

Yet even if we never discover the true identity of 'Hermes', one thing is certain: the country owes him an enormous debt of gratitude for alerting us to the hidden threat posed by the machinations of our elected leaders.

Andy Hamilton & Alistair Beaton
November 1980